The Elephant's Mouth

The Elephant's Mouth

Poems by

Luke Stromberg

© 2022 Luke Stromberg. All rights reserved.
This material may not be reproduced in any form, published,
reprinted, recorded, performed, broadcast,
rewritten or redistributed without
the explicit permission of Luke Stromberg.
All such actions are strictly prohibited by law.

Cover design by Shay Culligan
Cover image by Ana Tantaros
Author photograph by Ana Tantaros

ISBN: 978-1-63980-160-2

Kelsay Books
502 South 1040 East, A-119
American Fork, Utah 84003
Kelsaybooks.com

For My Father

Acknowledgments

I would like to extend my gratitude to the editors of the following publications in which some of these poems first appeared, often in different form.

823 on High: "A Man Interrogating a Rose"

Atavic Poetry: "Epithalamion"

Cassandra Voices: "The First Obscenity"

The Centrifugal Eye: "Talking to God," "Saturday Morning," "Chester Heights Camp Meeting"

Cleaver Magazine: "Memorial Day," "When I Sleep, I Dream of Tsunamis"

El Aleph Magazine: "The Wilderness"

E-Verse Radio: "Squirrel Luck," "Sestina," "New Year's Eve"

Goliad Review: "Risk," "Family First"

The Hopkins Review: "The Mugging," "Hard Hat"

The Mid-America Poetry Review: "On the Edge of Night"

The New Criterion: "The Elephant's Mouth"

Oddball Magazine: "A Dedication"

ONE ART: "Brain Tonic," "What I Want for Christmas"

The Philadelphia Inquirer: "Friends Southwestern Burial Ground," "On Being Twenty-Six in Your Hometown"

Philadelphia Stories: "The Bachelor"

The Raintown Review: "Personal Grooming"

Rotary Dial: "Patience," "Upper Darby"

Shot Glass Journal: "Rube"

Smartish Pace: "On Not Attending Church," "The Chimes at Midnight," "The American Experiment," "In Her Bedroom," "Lightning in the Rain"

Think Journal: "I'll Never Make it to Córdoba," "Visiting Hours," "Your Double"

Tower Journal: "Masked & Anonymous," "Visitor," and "Nobody but You"

The Turk's Head Review: "Abandoned Things"

Twelve Mile Review: "Night Hours"

The Victorian Violet Press Journal: "Renunciation"

"On the Edge of Night" won the 2007 Iris N. Spencer Undergraduate Award in Poetry and appears in *Iris N. Spencer Awards: The Early Years* (2014, Story Line Press).

"Black Thunder" was set to music by Melissa Dunphy for Network for New Music's Poetry Project in 2008. Dunphy's setting is for solo baritone, violin, cello, and piano. It was performed by Randall Scarlata, Paul Arnold, James Cooper III, and Linda Reichert at the

Kimmel Center in Philadelphia, PA on January 16, 2008. Dunphy also received Honorable Mention for the composition in the ASCAP/Lotte Lehman Foundation Art Song Competition in 2009.

"Patience" was featured on *Autumn Sky Poetry Daily* on March 17, 2017.

"Rube" and "Visiting Hours" were featured on the *HIV Here & Now Project* blog on March 14, 2016.

The cover image and my author photo were both taken by Ana Tantaros.

Many readers have offered their advice on drafts of these poems, and I want to express my sincere appreciation to them. Luke Bauerlein has been my most diligent reader, but I would also like to single out Alexander Long, Kate Northrop, Ernest Hilbert, Zach Burkhart, Kevin Cutrer, Kat Hayes, Matt Hayes, Elisabeth Majewski, John Velez, Chris Voght-Hennessy, Adam Wassel, and Christine Yurick.

My deepest thanks to Ned Balbo, John Wall Barger, Ernest Hilbert, and David Yezzi for carefully reading this manuscript and offering their invaluable advice.

I would be remiss if I did not also acknowledge the love and support that I received from my friends and family as I have tried my best to write poetry.

Special thanks should go to everyone involved in the West Chester University Poetry Conference, especially Michael Peich, Dana Gioia, Kim Bridgford, Sam Gwynn, Jesse Waters, Jamie Smith, and Cyndy Pilla. This book would not exist without West Chester.

Contents

I.

The Mugging	17
Personal Grooming	18
Patience	19
The Elephant's Mouth	20
Renunciation	23
Masked & Anonymous	24
The Bachelor	25
The Chimes at Midnight	26
On Being Twenty-Six in Your Hometown	28
I'll Never Make It to Córdoba	29

II.

New Year's Eve	33
Upper Darby	34
Chester Heights Camp Meeting	35
When I Sleep, I Dream of Tsunamis	37
The Wilderness	39
Memorial Day	41
Sestina	42

III.

The American Experiment	47
Black Thunder	48
What I Want for Christmas	49
Saturday Morning	51
Squirrel Luck	52
Talking to God	54
A Dedication	57

IV.

In Her Bedroom	61
Definitions	63
Your Double	64
Epithalamion	65
What the Crag Would Say	66
Abandoned Things	67
Lightning in the Rain	68
International Kissing Day (July 6)	69
Hard Hat	71

V.

Visitor	75
On the Edge of Night	76
Night Hours	77
A Man Interrogating a Rose	78
Bedroom	80
On Not Attending Church	81
Brain Tonic	83

VI.

Nobody but You	87
Family First	88
The First Obscenity	89
Visiting Hours	90
Rube	91
My Father's Hands	92
Friends Southwestern Burial Ground	93
Risk	94

I.

The Mugging

I had the muzzle of a gun, or something,
Pressed into the small of my back. "Your wallet,"
A voice demanded: dry, succinct—like breathing
In my naked ear, unasked, a secret.

As much as the gun, the robbery, his lifting
Out my wallet, himself, from my back pocket,
His hand's invasion, was what was violating.
After, the thought of that's what made me vomit.

My private world lost its private affect.
Now, even sitting in my kitchen alone,
I fear I cannot live my life apart.

For weeks, when walking from the El to home,
I've felt the condensation of his breath
Against my ear in the newly pregnant dark.

Personal Grooming

Three times a week, in a mask of foam, with a *Bic*
disposable razor in my hand, I search
for my face, scraping the stubble from my cheek.
The man I see, when I splash myself with water
and wipe the steam off of the mirror, could be me.
He stares back at me with a long and searching look.

This face I wear to work, the bank, or bar—that poses
for a photo with a smile summoned for the occasion—
is one I've found. I've seen it reflected in the eyes
of friends, teachers, women I took to bed—
I've learned a lot about myself from all of them,
read their letters of recommendation with weird greed.

Now, inspecting my face after a shave, a towel
wrapped jauntily around my shoulders, I'm surprised
by a sense of otherness from my own reflection
as if I'm meeting with some casual acquaintance:
a store clerk or someone who rides the bus with me.
And yet that scrubbed up face is me—at least for now.

Still, I can't help but imagine a wilder, stranger face.
Not the professor's face I show above the lectern—
bald and bespectacled, groomed and nervously polite—
but bearded almost to my naked blue eyes,
something much more like an ape or wolf,
a second animal face I can't quite disown.

Perhaps this Tarzan, whose face I shun, is the true me.
How could I know for sure? Not until some Jane,
lost among the tangled vines of a foreign jungle,
her English lady's dress soaked through with sweat,
finds him there beneath the high canopy,
and smiles, calling him by my name.

Patience

His ears set back, his eyes fixed on the dark
Beneath the radiator, the cat crouches,
Glimpsing whiskers there, two feet, a nose.
And when a mouse decides to test the light—
Sniffing the kitchen air—he rises higher
On his haunches—But he doesn't pounce.
Instead, he allows it to escape, tail twitching
Behind it, back into the dark, untried.

Reckless, he waits. Patience is also risk.
And though it may not seem this way to most,
That takes real nerve: letting a chance slip past,
Believing that a better one will come.
Meanwhile, the pretzel bag's chewed full of holes.
Turds are on the counter. The mouse, alive.

The Elephant's Mouth

"What's it take to join the circus?" my father asked.
A gang of workers were putting up a tent,
Big hammers ringing on the pegs in rhythm.
"I'm thinking that I'd like to join up with you guys."

This was '45 or there about I'd guess
When the circus used to come to town each year.
My father was just a boy then, eight or nine.
Their train would rumble past his house on Guilford Road.

"Well, to join the circus," one offered, "you gotta be brave."
He leaned on his hammer and mopped his brow with his shirt.
"Are you brave, Kid?" he asked, appraising my father,
Who, conscious of the chuckling men, answered, "I'm brave."

"Enough to stick your head up in an elephant's mouth?"
The workers gathered, happy for a break.
"I ain't afraid," he said, a bit less certain.
"Well, come on then—I know just the elephant!"

The animal was penned up in a tent nearby.
Pulling back the flap, the man said, "You're sure?"
"I'm sure," my father said, not sure at all,
Not when he saw it stamp its mud-splattered feet.

Held by his knees, my father was raised up to its mouth,
And he did it—stuck his head inside—
To the delight of all the roaring men.
Then eyes shut tight, pulled free, his bravery made clear.

Whatever my father felt inside that creature's mouth
I'll never know. I've looked at elephants
Chewing grass or slack-jawed in repose
And wondered: Is it hot in there? Do they have teeth?

"My eyes were closed," my father says, "I can't remember."
I try to place myself within that tent.
"You weren't even *thought of* then!" he laughs.
"I was a different person. So much has happened since."

He thinks they said that he should come back when he was older,
That he was Grade A circus material,
And gave him passes to the show that night,
Which must have been at least a little disappointing.

How does a kid go back to St. Cyril's after that?
Desks of unworldly children blotting ink,
A sister with her yardstick in the aisle,
The wide blackboard that seemed to bar the way to fun.

Within a few brief days, the tents were all brought down,
And then the neighborhood was taken back
By normal people and their normal tasks;
No snake-skinned man walked to the corner store for smokes.

One of the hardest things I've ever had to do
Was to let go of my belief—long held—
That I was set apart for something special,
Blessed by distinction like a high-wire trapeze artist.

And, to be honest, I'm not sure I have let go:
The illustrated woman haunts my nights
With promises of some lost and unclaimed life.
I have to will myself to go to work each day.

But sometime in his twenties, my father married my mother.
He sold his red hot-rod convertible,
And then acquired a mortgage and raised five boys.
For thirty some odd years, he worked for the school district.

Today, my father lives just blocks from Guilford Road.
No tent has gone up in the field for decades.
The train line that ran through is long since gone.
And he hardly can remember that elephant at all.

Renunciation

I never lived the life I left behind.
I never strolled down leafy avenues,
past blue mailboxes and garden tulips, or stood on a lawn
playing a guitar and singing to a girl in a window,
so there was no loss. I watched the green world
wither into brown and burn in a frenzy.
I brushed its ashes from my coat.
It never told the truth, anyway.
I gave up that life for the coughing city,
its wheezing pedestrians and congested streets,
for a sky swollen with rain, a newspaper
blowing down the road.
                                      So now I live in a shadow.
Friends drop by in gloves, hats, and scarves
to ruin the snow with their footprints.
And when they speak, their breath blooms
before their mouths and vanishes.
I'm left to my quieted mind,
free of wounding smiles, the weight of possibility.
But once in a while, I look to the east
and see the morning break behind the trees,
and, for a moment, I become aware of a ghost,
sharing my body, the ghost of someone I thought was gone,
a man who never existed.

Masked & Anonymous

She's got everything she needs
She's an artist, she don't look back
—Bob Dylan, "She Belongs to Me"

Tonight, he looks like a stately cattle rancher,
a Southern gentleman in a tailored suit,
as he bows, almost shyly, to his audience.
But when he smiles, a rare gift, he becomes,
for a haunted moment, the wild haired boy
with the guitar and odd device around his neck
from a thousand black and white photographs.

What must it be like, to do that to a crowd?
The short bursts of harmonica,
the voice perfected by cigarettes:
They are so rich with our own memories.
He is a man who lives in his own shadow,
whose excellence hangs over him, a curse.
It must be lonely to be so loved.

Passing a diner and looking through the window,
he'll see the people at the tables—chatting,
stirring their coffee, buttering their toast—
and know that, if he entered, took down his hood,
that they might suddenly forget how to act.
And when someone approaches, nervously, to ask,
'Excuse me, are you—*him?*', he has to wonder, 'Am I?'

But still you'll find him on the road,
standing in the hot glare of the stage,
just a ticket away, yet still elusive:
Flickering a dozen different faces
and singing for no one but himself,
squinting into the lights, his eyes like slits,
his lips pulled back, showing his teeth.

The Bachelor

We imagine him sexless—this wifeless,
childless man with his false teeth and crushed hat,
each article of clothing a different
species of plaid, as if he hailed from a time
before the invention of mirrors.
It's easy for us to imagine him
on an afternoon walk, or home alone
in his armchair, his ancient TV set
like a Rembrandt, the picture surrounded
by encroaching darkness. He seems never
to have been young. One hears how he spent years
caring for his mother, while his sisters
married, raised families—his own life a mere
sub-plot. And this image makes sense to us.
But you'll forgive me if I picture him
young, in bed with a woman, also young.
It's Sunday morning, and he doesn't care
that he's not at Mass. The birds are singing.
She turns her face to his and smiles, her cheek
against her pillow, her breath sweet and warm.
The strap of her nightgown's off her shoulder,
a softness in her eyes that says she knows him.
This is what his life had to offer.
This is his story, the one he'll tell
himself over and over. Who else will
remember it? The way the light shone behind
the blinds, the way they had no money
and bickered all the time—the way he loved her.

The Chimes at Midnight

For Leo James Stromberg

You ranted; you raved. You handled life too rough.
Bartenders' eyes would glare with homicide.
Alright, they'd say, *I think you've had enough.*
Thrown out of every bar you stepped inside,

And taunted, mocked, subdued by burly cops,
You couldn't rouse this fallen world to listen.
But like an express train blowing past your stops,
You raged, intent upon a holy mission.

In record shops or diners, you'd testify
How cheapskates and bouncers would one day be judged
To strangers who'd listen and think, *Who is this guy?*
You had your principles and never budged.

Stout as a tree stump, bearded and long-haired,
A Viking raider out of central casting,
The thunder-bolt scar on your forehead flared
When you would get yourself into a passion.

*The Lord would rather us be poor than slaves
To "things,"* you'd roar. *Resist the alarm clock crowd!*
Their fancy homes, their boats, their cars were graves.
The well-heeled in the churches were all too proud.

We fought; we laughed. We stupefied ourselves
With endless tokes and talked delicious nonsense
While Neil Young's high and plaintive voice wove spells.
Back then, I was still in my innocence

And half believed that it was possible
To live exempt forever. I was wrong.
I found a job and married as people will.
You're six years gone. It doesn't feel that long.

You were a nut—but, ah! the nights we had!
Yes, we heard the chimes at midnight, my friend,
Another round, our motto, for good or bad,
And drank as if the night would never end.

On Being Twenty-Six in Your Hometown

While stranded in traffic, she thought how she was trapped,
Beset by cars of desperate commuters,
The sun, on distant buildings, a watchfire's glow.
Beyond them, in the dreamed of world of change,
A girl, much like herself, was making good,
But she feared she might never move, might die
There locked in her car, with Billy Joel still on.
Three crows perched on a dumpster seemed to wait…

Well, anyway, she lived. Thank God for that.
But that feeling of being stuck—stopped, prevented
From becoming the girl she swore she was,
Remained all night so that she felt behind
The wheel still, still strapped in for that long ride
That took her nowhere and never brought her back.

I'll Never Make It to Córdoba

Inspired by Federico Garcia Lorca's "Cancion de jinete"

Córdoba.
Distant and alone.

Wednesday evening, well past midnight.
My neighbor's television through the wall.
No one sleeps these days.
Though I know the way—
across the ocean in Andalusia—
I'll never make it to Córdoba.

Streets wait to be wandered,
conversations to be had, drinks to be served.
A guitarist tunes his instrument.
The gypsy girl passes through a curtain of beads,
her skirt wrapped around her.
On a dark red sofa, she listens
for the sound of a bell,
a voice on the intercom.
Somewhere in Córdoba.

My days are ruined by work.
My nights have too many hours.
This life does not belong to me.
I watch my shadow
like a movie on the wall.

Outside, Death, leaning against a parking meter,
drags on a cigarette.
I peer through the shade.
He nods, flicks the butt,
takes a stroll, hands in his pockets.
But I know he'll be back
before I make it to Córdoba.

An empty cup, a chip along the rim,
a radio talk show, the volume turned down.
I rub the stubble on my cheek.
On the wall, a map of Spain—
its edges brown with age—
a pin pushed through Córdoba,
distant and alone.

II.

New Year's Eve

It'll never be 1999 again.
The photo on your old I.D. won't bring it back
Nor the mix tape found buried in a dresser drawer,
Your handwriting in faded ink on its label.

You'll never be the kid that made that tape again.
That skinny boy is lost like a dead relative
Or an ancient screen siren, Art Deco sexy
In a shimmering gown that was once all elegance.

Though the past was misery once, we've learned to forget.
Now it's a pang. We crave a love that's long gone sour,
Find tears for a home gladly left, grow fond of dolts.
This year, too, is already almost history:

Its crises, its talk show punch lines near obsolete.
It's likely you'll never know its real charm until
It's just one more thing that won't be back, like pay phones
In the mall or encyclopedia salesmen.

You wait for midnight like Gary Cooper waiting
In *High Noon* for a train he'd rather wouldn't come,
Your friends flushed with drink and smooching on the sofa,
That strange looking year printed on their paper hats.

No longer thin, no longer very young either,
You don't know who you're supposed to be anymore.
In time, you'll learn, but you'll always miss that feeling
Of *home*—a feeling that you only think you've felt.

Upper Darby

I'm caught in you like a swamp.
You lie, a tangle of lives,
West of Philadelphia,
A secret nobody keeps.
Neighborhoods like Babylon's
After its tower toppled:
A flurry of different tongues
Thrown together in one place
Where old Greeks sing in gardens
Among tall tomato plants
And Sikhs crowd the gurdwara,
Confusing all the bigots.
Hometown of row homes and playgrounds
Squared by chain-link fences,
Of sandwich shops and taverns,
Your train tracks and maple trees
Have grown entwined with my life.
My uncle's squad car cruises
Out of the past, down these blocks.
It's always still happening:
That empty pizzeria
Is where my parents will meet,
Long Lane is still in its prime.
I'll die on 69th Street
In front of a Foot Locker
Or wig shop, clutching my chest
From the heart attack that killed
My granddad at the Exxon
On Marshall, before the flood.

Chester Heights Camp Meeting

What you'll remember, like I do,
is the smell of fallen leaves, of smoke on a blanket,
things I can't separate
from the place to this day—
in the same way I can't separate
metal washing basins or wood crosshatching
from the summers we spent there.
You'll remember the spiral staircase
with its threadbare carpeting—
charming in its oddity— and the dead
chipmunks Tiger would leave for us
beside our beds— a new one each morning—
to step on with bare feet.

But the cottages. The painted trim.
Wooden shutters. Outhouses in back.
Colored lights strung around balconies.
None of these belonged to me anymore.
They belonged to someone else—some other boy.
You must have felt the same way.

Behind the screen, full of holes
we used to poke our fingers through,
the door to our cottage was locked,
the keys in Mr. Montgomery's pocket.
He was nodding gravely, talking to Dad,
who was smiling, of course, joking
in the private language of adults
we were only beginning to understand
as we sat in the back seat of Dad's old sedan,
and I squinted at the cover
of a Captain America comic
that refused to come into focus.

I've left something behind there, something
less obvious than my initials
carved into the soft wood of the bedroom door,
something I could never locate in any other place.
But I took something with me as well:
the sense of loss one must develop
and perfect as one grows older—
as you and I have, away from childish games—
something that—if it had a sound—
might sound like the tires of Dad's car
crunching the gravel drive for the last time,
the black dog—Whose dog? Where did it come from?—
that chased the car, barking.

When I Sleep, I Dream of Tsunamis

I'm walking down Garrett Road when a blue
and strangely beautiful tidal wave rises
in the distance, reaching high over rooftops.

It's the sound of wind, of water
gathering force,
that I hear first,

and I cannot move,
awed by this wall of ocean
that seems to come from nowhere

as its shadow falls over an afternoon scene:
       a meter-maid writing a ticket;
       two teenagers skipping school;
       a store clerk sweeping;
       a man walking his dog.
They all seem to notice at once.

I run, my legs heavy
with the thought
of what's behind me . . .

                    And I'm ditched someplace
I've never been, lying
in a puddle
on a deserted street.

Old bicycles, women's clothing, church pews,
shattered bits of wood
scattered all around me—
but not one person

when I get up, inexplicably dry,
trembling, amazed
that I can stand,
breathe, that my mouth and lungs
haven't filled with water

and look around,
the sun glorious.

The Wilderness

The wilderness is coming soon.
The city has been undermined.
The street lights will go dead in protest.
The faces of the row houses
Will be shamed, obscured by ivy
As grass grows through cracks in the pavement.
Dogs, mangy and unwashed, will roam free
Down roads blanched with moonlight
While owls watch from chimney tops,
And the graffiti squirms to life
And flies away like a swarm of locusts
To some distant harvest.

People will stay up late,
Sitting on front porches, drinking moonshine
And listening to crickets sing
In yards they now refuse
To mow ever again,
The men shirtless, the women sleek,
Hungry, nearly naked,
Hair windblown, wild and lovely.

And sometime later, perhaps, long after
The traffic lights have ceased their flashing,
The people, with their soft flesh,
Grasping hands, and laughter
Will be forgotten like good sense,
The apartment houses stocked with rotting bones,
The business district still,
Old neighborhoods lush and green,
Stinking of prosperity.

It's going to happen
Soon. Very soon.
Just the other day, off Market Street,
In the shadow of the El, I saw a deer
Stepping through grass strewn
With fast-food debris and shredded plastic bags,
Staring blankly into traffic, almost as if
She belonged there.

Memorial Day

When you were a boy, did you dream that street
And wonder where it was? Did you dream
Of death in an exotic locale?
Iraq—its bicycles and minarets. Its men
And their sweat-shined, mustached faces
On the television. Women in the hijab,
Weeping in debris. Did your temples throb
In its dry desert heat? A roadside bomb,
Assembled there—in that ancient, wasted place—
Scheduled you and others for oblivion,
Claimed you, even then in Conshohocken.

We've never met and never will,
But this afternoon, I sit at a picnic table
Under a tree with my brother and nephew
And think of you. The street parked up
On both sides for a soccer game.
Cheers rise harmlessly above our music.
Strangers here are less strange.
Nothing is quite mysterious—
Even the shadow pattern of the branches
On the walkway. This is the life I know.
And, for you, I wonder: would I die for even this?

Sestina

I keep telling myself that they're only harmless dreams,
But every night I learn that these are empty words.
They're there again, in the cemetery across the street—
Policemen, their sirens flashing red in the dark
as they dig up graves. I know they're searching
for something to accuse me of. And they laugh—

I can't tell you how many times I've heard them laugh
late into the night. They pursue me through my dreams,
ghouls in blue uniforms that never tire of searching.
Pleading my innocence is useless. There are no words.
They trap me in their lights as they pass me in the dark
and smile, their squad cars creeping down the street.

I have to look over my shoulder, walking down the street.
Down an alley I hear a dusty laugh
but see only an outline, the glimmer of a badge in the dark.
My life has been invaded by my dreams.
The sides of buildings are covered with illegible words
addressed to policemen, constantly searching.

I worry what they might uncover with their searching.
They say I killed a man on the street—
left him lying dead. I can't accept their words.
I protest, call them liars, but they only laugh.
I tell them that it happened in my dreams,
and how can I help what I envision in the dark?

They gather "evidence" against me, working well past dark.
Their whole lives are devoted to their searching.
I've become deathly afraid of my dreams.
A surveillance van is parked a little down the street
Where they've been listening to my calls. I should laugh,
but it isn't funny. I'm paranoid about my words—

That they may somehow convict me with my own words.
Who knows what they might overhear in the dark?
They might plant some drugs. It makes me sick how they'll laugh
if I accidentally confess to something. Their searching
is driving me crazy! They're across the street,
digging up bones of people I've never met—even in my dreams.

The clocks all laugh. Both day and night are dark.
My tormentors are searching through my words for bloodstains.
I am followed down every street I walk down in my dreams.

III.

The American Experiment

Even now a woman threatens to enter this poem.
I am at my desk with only the light
of my small lamp for company, composing
an ode to the American experiment
when she rings my bell. There she is:
a bottle of Merlot under her arm, wearing
a raincoat, heels, and—she claims—nothing else.
Oh, how I long to be a serious-minded person!

Egypt this week has seen a revolution.
I want to bring the revolution here, to this room.
This poem demands a free and democratic Luke Stromberg!
I will not be ruled by solipsism. Like Christ
in the desert, tempted into lust and trifles,
I choose instead a higher purpose. Already
my words inspire action: I give the woman cab fare,
send her home.

          I pick up my pen, close my eyes,
imagine an end to war and begin to write it down.
But from my rooms, the world looks wet and blurred—
the familiar rooftops, the market, the headlights of cars.
In my store-bought yellow light, I am small
and petty. Mideast unrest, climate change—
they bore me, shallow aesthete that I am.
And so I rise to look for her taxi in the streetlights.

Why fight it? This poem belongs to her.

Black Thunder

It was late. Her light was the only light
that could be seen from the street below.
I held some drugstore roses, standing
in her doorway, a useless grin on my face.
She smiled sympathetically
and looked away.

Last night, I drank until my head
roared with black thunder.
I staggered home, feeling lost.
Two dogs whispered gossip to each other.
Somewhere sirens wailed like ghosts.
I lay down on my floor
and watched the ceiling fan spin
when it wasn't on.

When the days pile up, like dishes
in the sink, I start to panic,
lost in the rooms of my imagination.
She sounds very bored when we talk,
every smile a secret sneer.
My brain whirls like a table-saw.

What I Want for Christmas

One of those women who jump out of cakes.

She would be scandalously young, preferably—
twenty-one or twenty-two—
And—what the hell—let's make her a blonde,
one that looks good
in a white bikini bottom
and has a flat tummy.
That'd work.

Nah. Not really.

I wouldn't know what to do with her.
We'd probably end up friends.
She would look up to me.
Later, she'd introduce me to her boyfriend, Kyle.
He'd be a guy in a sleeveless t-shirt
who likes to call me "Bro."
Most likely he'd look up to me, too.

How about a swordfish, then,
or one of those big, goofy moose heads
to mount on the wall above my fireplace?
But I actually don't have a fireplace—
so one of those, too.
And some logs to burn in my fireplace.
And a velvet jacket and a mug of grog.
And a high-backed leather chair to drink my grog in.

A Model-T Ford.
A scarf, a pair of gloves, some goggles.
A submarine.

A fleet of bicyclists.
A typewriter
possessed by the soul of an alcoholic playwright.

Or someone I could talk to.
(The nights are long and dark this time of year.)

Someone who makes me laugh, who finds
something debonair about a man in glasses.
She could have red hair and smooth skin, too,
the whitest teeth,
a way of sighing to herself
she probably doesn't even know about.

There's a good movie playing downtown.
Maybe she'd like to go.

Saturday Morning

I roam the streets,
like a rabid dog,
a diseased sex maniac,
something off in my gait.
I grind my teeth
down blocks of sun-drenched lawns,
hoping for an innocent out for a stroll—
the violence of her body
concealed beneath a cotton dress.

From the safety of her kitchen,
a housewife pushes aside
a curtain, decorated with stalks of corn,
and gasps to see me in her garden,
smelling the flowers, fondling them
with my dirty fingers.

Soon the police arrive
in a black-and-white, gleaming
with menace in the summer sun.
They spy me in the distance,
my feet dangling above
the ground, as I climb a tree
to get a better look at a girl.

I am caught in their rifle scope.
And I fall,
shot in the back, put down
like a rabid dog,
a diseased sex maniac.
I lie on the grass,
coughing blood. And the girl
passes by a window in just her bra.

Squirrel Luck

I can't sleep.
The squirrels are fucking
again—in my wall.
I can hear them:
nails across wood,
excited chatter,
then, finally, a sound I imagine
as the female's sigh of satisfaction—
over and over.
They fuck
all night long.
The whole world is fucking.

I picture the young couple next door—
the husband
steely-eyed, square-jawed—
his thin, blond wife,
fond of yoga pants
and jogging—writhing
on bed sheets, their tanned bodies
all muscle and sweat, making love
in the blue glow of their television set—
and I hate them.

It's a kind of luck to be born a squirrel,
dumb to all the menace of sex.
They live free from dignity
and—if they're lucky—
exit dramatically,
plummeting from a leafy tree-top
to the street, crushed
beneath the wheels of an Oldsmobile,

transformed into a gray and red splatter
that curious children come to poke with sticks.
Squirrels never suffer, not really.
If you ever look into their vacant, black eyes,
you will know this is true.

Talking to God

I am a brother to dragons and a companion to owls.
God, I'm being melodramatic—forgive me.
I've been having a hard time lately.
My friends have all been replaced by empty chairs.
Some mornings I feel weak as a wet paper bag.
The spring's long days and yellow leaves are too far off.
I wonder if they will come again.

God, let me be simple and happy
Like the people in Pepsi ads.
Pull this frowning face off me as if it were a rubber mask.
I feel something clawing at my heart,
Like fingers grubbing in the dirt,
And as I stop to think, the end of my pen in my mouth,
I realize I have no idea who I am.

A visionary? A flake? A reprobate?
The kind of man they erect statues of in parks?
Or a ragged hidalgo, tilting at windmills?
Surely, I'm not one of the numberless in between, standing in line
    at the DMV, same haircuts, same clothes.
Am I moving toward something, someone, slowly turning to gold?
Or stranded in my living room, watching daytime television?
I feel like the understudy for myself.

It's time for something new.
God, I've always admired Humphrey Bogart.
Give me his peculiar grace, his fast-talk;
Let me stand with one hand in my pocket, swirling scotch in a
    snifter, calling some woman "Kid,"
A tough guy, blowing smoke between my lips, fazed by nothing.

Thank You, God, by the way, for smoke on black and white film,
    curling, like ivy up a wall, from a cigarette resting in a
    jeweled ashtray.
If only cigarettes didn't cause cancer, I'd smoke two packs a day.

God, sometimes I want to die—
But let it be peacefully in my sleep
Or after collapsing on my lawn in my bathrobe while getting the
    morning paper, something swift and easy.
Spare me the ugly farewell:
The solemn young doctor with his clipboard,
My family, the sick bed.
I don't like the thought of brownish blood streaking my clean,
    white, porcelain sink.

God, let me be noteworthy.
Don't let me blend in with the wallpaper this time.
It would be nice to be admired, to matter,
To have my own talk show with potted plants, a sidekick.
Let me mock myself on stage before a dark, laughing crowd;
Maybe the floodlights will burn away my insecurity.
God, you should have never let me watch television.

This body you've given me—pale and thin, like some ascetic—is
    no use to me.
I am as welcome on the beach as an oil spill.
Don't let that brute in the tight swim trunks kick sand in my face.
God, introduce me to Charles Atlas; make me famous for my
    build.
I am so tired of women who say they love my mind.
I want to be loved for my body.
I don't want to be just friends.

I want to inspire lust in a mousey librarian with cat-eye glasses.
Allow me to slowly unbutton her blouse.
Don't make my fingers tremble; let me kiss her white throat and feel her breath against my ear.
God, I want the cheerleaders, too.
I want them to lie awake weeping for me, burying their faces in pillows.
Let it please, *please*, be the other way around for a change,
As I offer an apology, my voice pained, the faintest gleam of triumph in my eyes.

God, allow some darling's heart to open to me.
Make me appeal to more than just her vanity.
I am through with trying to meet women in supermarkets.
I'd like to delete my OkCupid account.
God, I know I want too much.
This morning I saw the silhouette of a hawk perched in a tree, crows circling around it.
I wanted my desires to go with that hawk into the distance.

God, in the early morning hours, a small bird comes and pecks at my lips.
It is the Holy Spirit—I know it.
I am trying my best.
I've heard how you've transformed men who had exhausted their means: their eyes red, drugs all gone, money spent, no longer able to fake transcendence.
Am I really such a lost case?
I'm not on my knees, but I'm praying. Really. I can start going to church again.
God, I'm ready; touch me, please;
                                  teach me to surrender.

A Dedication

I am surrounded by women.
A cocktail party is in progress:
laughter, the clinking of glasses,
conversations blending into one steady drone.
A brunette gracefully wields an unlit cigarette
between two fingers like a threat, always
on the verge of lighting up,
and speaks excitedly about work.
In a chair on the other side of the room,
a black-eyed blonde crosses her legs,
looks around, bored.
She sips from a flute of champagne.

Someone laughs shrilly. A drink spills.
The room fills up with fog.
The women become indistinct, a crowd
of chattering shadows.
The starlight is locked out.
I'm closed in.
I open my mouth to speak
and produce a sound like shattering glass.

You out there, in the night, somewhere,
maybe sitting in your car at a red light, alone,
turn on your radio—
You might hear my song.

IV.

In Her Bedroom

I envy men who sleep without my trouble
in women's bedrooms, covet their hard hearts
or luck: their blind hours filled with lithesome girls
whose youthful breasts flatten while they lie
down on their backs and smile, polite as strangers.

Lust is a symptom, I know, and sex no cure
for bone-deep boredom. Still, I admire that brand
of sinner, sleeping on damp sheets beside
a long and naked girl I cannot win
even in my dreams. The *guilt*. Just think:

no fear, no jealousy, no promises
beyond a late-night clutch of passion. Nothing
but pure pleasure. No thinking, just the rush.
They leave their hearts someplace to rot, believe
that they're as weightless as a morning fog.

But in a woman's bed tonight, I think
of all the ways that we could hurt each other.
Sodden with the stubborn ethics of sex,
I listen to her shower run and worry:
did my whiskers scrape her face again?

The careless pleasure seekers stay well hidden,
while I lie like a kill on pastel sheets,
nestled in pillows and her down comforter,
trying to reclaim my sense of self,
her lacy curtains hung against the light.

Beyond that window, the world is waiting, vast
and eager to involve me in its ballgames
and industry. My car below us, vacant.
When she returns, her towel is half unwrapped,
her smile tender and intolerable.

Definitions

Luck is coming home
late in the evening
and finding a naked woman asleep in my bed.
She's lying on her stomach,
her hands tucked under a pillow,
with her long, black hair
curling down the center of her back.

Foolishness is what draws me away
from her, back into the moonlight,
to pace and search the sky for a brighter star.
Indecision: the space between us,
the untouched, nervous minutes
between me and whatever it is
that I actually want from life.

Courage, I've learned, is an old knight
stranded on top of a pyramid
a million miles away from me.
Sometimes we talk on a ham radio.
He offers me encouragement,
his voice broken by static.
I try to summon him to my side

While *Time,* which is, of course, a river,
rushes past me into an ocean called *Loss.*
And what am *I?* I can't decide
whether I am a cartoon detective,
purposely bungling his case,
or a farmer, during a hungry winter,
holding tightly to a prayer.

Your Double

She was a different woman I knew last year,
one without your flair for intimacy;
your black eyes glitter like a chandelier
now when you take my arm to walk beside me.
And yet, the resemblance is very much still there.
The way a joke causes your mouth to tighten,
the dimple in your cheek, the style you wear
your hair: they call to mind that other woman.
One night it was as if she left the room
and sent you in her place, with deeper eyes
and darker voice, misted with perfume.
But still, I get these doubts I can't disguise:
We'll touch sometimes, and, suddenly, I'll remember
some slight from her and then not feel as tender.

Epithalamion

Today let's put aside our cynicism.
The girl who searched all night, asking the watchmen
For news of her love gone missing, finally has found him,
So, just this once, we can believe again.
The boy can rest, his heart at peace.
Let all the vanquished angels find the voice
We thought they lost and foul now turn to fair.
So all the saps that failed at love may find redress,
Alert the sun to burn the smoggy air
And fill this church to prove to them
That sometimes we are allowed a chance to win.
For love may be soft knocking at your door
Or may come hard like rain that swells the air all summer
Then teems on roofs in thrashing wind and thunder,
But love is not too much to ask for.
And though these lovers, like us, know nothing for sure,
The purpose of this hour is understood:
Today he gives his life to her to change, for good.

What the Crag Would Say

The waves crash against my face,
but I do not feel them.
The cold does not disturb me.
I have no compassion for the souls
dashed upon my body.
That couple on the beach—
her raised voice, his hands thrown up
when she turns her back to him—
I do not know what they are feeling.
I do not know what it is like
to lie awake with a storm in my head.
I do not fear the long night.
I do not fear at all.

Abandoned Things

The memory of you is scum that clings
to what you left behind, abandoned things.
Your schmaltzy records by singers I abhor
are piled like overdue bills by my door;
your lotions clutter up my cabinet;
your "favorites" greet me on the Internet—
And when I go out, must I always see
a friend of yours who recognizes me
from some party I attended, once, with you?
And must they always ask about you, too?
Your name is like a bruise left on my arm
I carry with me like a luckless charm.
These walls still hold the echo of your laugh
as if that sound were now our epitaph,
but it's so faint I have to strain to hear it—
I have to strain so very hard to hear it.

Lightning in the Rain

And just like that, it's like nothing happened,
as if you dreamed the warm spot she left
in your bed, the press of her hand on your arm.
The house forgets. From the kitchen,
where your voices used to blend in talk,
from the rooms that held the medicine of her presence,
only a loud, persistent monotone:
a silence that seems to have a voice.
All joy is just a flash of lightning in the rain.
You cannot believe otherwise.

And on your way to work you see,
on the roadside, a dead deer,
the asphalt smeared with blood and tire tracks,
the animal twisted, its neck bent back,
so that it stares with no light in its eyes
as drivers zip past and, almost, forget themselves.
And you want the clouds to look like smoke from ruins,
but they only look like clouds. And the old woman
who waits at the intersection for the bus
does not know who you are.

International Kissing Day (July 6)

Miserable, again.
Here it is, International Kissing Day,
And I can't even get a peck on the cheek
From the woman I miss.
It's always been the longing for a kiss
That kept me up at night:
The way a face looked
Turned up beneath a streetlight,
Fingers on my sleeve,
My hand on a hip,
A smile. A smile
That's not for me—
Not again. Listen:

The pearly whites of lovers on a tube of toothpaste,
Their mouths so intimate,
Banged me up at seven, left me with an ache
Not in my tooth but deeper.
I had to kiss or break.
That was in the eighties.
I still feel the same
As an over forty creeper.
Kid, these twenty-first century girls
Have teeth you wouldn't believe.
I cup my mouth with my hand.
My breath is never fresh—
Their faces always are.

Love is an advanced case of Stockholm Syndrome.
Her smile's a bear trap,
Her laugh a nail gun,
And I'm snarled up in her.

It's no use. I cry
When someone tries to set me loose.
Please don't try.
Okay, I'll admit it:
I'm obsessed with *sex*.
My head's a wreck.
I sent her a text:
Happy Kissing Day—
My lips are chapped.

Hard Hat

This morning, on the bus, I saw that man again,
the guy in the hard hat. I can never figure out
why he wears that thing—surely not for any *job*,
not this guy. His eyes have that glassy look,
like he's dazed. You just know his breath stinks.
What's his name? No one asks. Better to just sit back,
feel sorry for the girl in the nurse's scrubs
he leans toward, saying, "I like your hair. I like hair."

He sat apart today, rocking back and forth,
scratching at his eyebrows like he was trying
to un-see some mistake, and tapping on his hat.
A woman sat across from him. She turned to me
with this smirk—and it felt like a reprieve.
Because I was thinking, then, of how I'd keep calling you,
of the thin, plaintive ringing without answer
that summer you left me for another man.

V.

Visitor

I open wide my door at night.
The cold is like the cold of space.
You stand alone across the street.
The wind catches your coat, your scarf.

You smile, call out to me, and laugh.
I cannot hear your voice from here.
In the outer air, the falling snow,
Your voice is gone. The darkness has it.

A car is idling on the corner,
A flume of fragrant exhaust behind it.
Someone's footprints in the yard.
They are not mine. They are not yours.

On the Edge of Night

The dogs are barking at the edge of night.
The trees are black, the sky a frosty gray.
We are no longer sure of what is right.

Our prayers can only reach a certain height.
They struggle in the air and go astray
While dogs keep barking at the edge of night.

The church's spire is not a welcome sight.
The preacher's sermons have become passé.
We are no longer sure of what is right.

God's angels fold their wings and hide their light
From those who listen for their harps to play
But hear only dogs at the edge of night.

We wonder why our lives have lost their bite.
The past is lost, so lonely, so far away.
We seem to have forgotten what is right.

Yet still I come back to my desk to write
My songs, though they die in the mouth of day.
Though dogs are barking at the edge of night,
I have not lost my taste for what is right.

Night Hours

My digital clock shines red and bleary
        as the eyes of a drunk.
Light from a street lamp
        breaks through my blinds.

I think of the individual lives
        closed up in houses on narrow streets,
the eyes that stare
        from cars stuck in traffic jams;
imagine the secret lives
        of those blond prisoners of beauty;
the morgue's inventory of cold bodies
        with purple gun-shot wounds;
the bitterness on the lips of comedians.

People make love
        as if they were parts in a machine,
and men in high offices
        make decisions about the weather,
while the nightclub singer, full of tears,
        abandons her microphone.

My sleep is fitful
        and full of black, circling birds.

A Man Interrogating a Rose

Bent over a flower bed, poised
above a rose. I watch him,
looking like he's some sad tourist:
khaki shorts, sandals, a three-day beard,
a Panama hat shading his eyes.
He caresses the petals
like you would touch a girl's cheek.
His lips move, but I can't hear him.
Is he whispering love-words to this rose?

Or does he, like us, have questions?
What's it like to always
have to keep your head up?
Why does twilight in autumn
taste like apples?
How is it that my wife's hands
can get so cold?
Does he expect this rose, of all roses,
to listen? Care?

That's a damned odd thing to do:
to talk to a flower, to ask a rose
whose voice that is
trapped in the wind
or why, in that not-too-far-off,
Death waits with a sick grin
and morning breath
like a pastor by the doors
at the end of a service.

We all find a reason
to get up in the morning:
the kids' drive to school,

that girl at the Starbucks,
baseball, rock n roll, money . . .
We all want it to mean something.

On Monday, in an office
with cheap, fluorescent light,
I will feed dozens
of yellowing pages—
memos, construction plans:
records of other men's work—
one by one into a scanner
where they will be saved on a computer
as crude images, never to be consulted
and probably forgotten.
I've been doing this for months—
And yet I have the nerve to ask
why anyone would talk to a rose.

Bedroom

During the night without
Quite slipping out of sleep
I become aware
Of how empty my room is
There seems to be a great expanse
Of open air around me
And it frightens me the edge
Of my mattress hanging
Slightly off the bed
To think I could be lost
In such vastness I could
Fall and never land

On Not Attending Church

Church, I'm sad to say, is boring.
I can admit it now.
All that up and down for listless singing
Over blaring organ music,
The pastor straining at the pulpit:
It feels a little less than sacred.

We sat up in the balcony—
My family and I—
In a row of aluminum folding chairs
Most Sundays of my younger years.
I felt a sense of duty then
That lingers as a guilty feeling

When I sleep until eleven
On Sunday mornings now.
I'll still show up for Christmas Eve or Easter
To stick a twenty in the plate
And wonder why God's famous Grace
Hasn't swelled my meager heart,

But I stay greedy with my life.
I asked my dad one time,
As he stood shaving by the bathroom mirror,
What Heaven would be like.
He stirred his razor in murky water
And told me, "No one really knows, Son,

But we'll all be together there—
You, me, your mom, your brothers—
And we'll rejoice and praise God's name forever,
Knowing that He loves us all—
Doesn't that sound wonderful?"
—It sounded a lot like church to me.

I pictured the saints in folding chairs
Or crowding wooden pews—
A service lasting an eternity
Without a cookout to look forward to—
And tried to hide my disappointment,
My feeling that there must be more.

I've always wanted something more—
From church, from work, from love—
Too often my life resembles a tasteless meal:
I pick away, feeling bored,
Pretending that I'm satisfied,
And leave the table hungry still.

But surely, it's better to go to church
Than watch the Sunday shows…
Who knows? The Hound of Heaven may catch me yet.
I read red-lettered text with longing,
Hoping that it finally will.
Meanwhile, the boring churches wait.

Brain Tonic

for John Foy

Like my grandmother before me, I like to drink
A refreshing can of Coca Cola for breakfast.
It's part of my arrested development.
Sadly, I never developed a taste for coffee,
A classic marker of maturity,
Like when a girl gets her first training bra.
I do enjoy the occasional hot tea
(With too much sugar and milk), but I prefer
To keep it low class. Don't misunderstand—
It's not a political gesture, just my "truth."
I find the initial sip of carbonated
Sweetness akin to the lost ritual
Of that first frosty-morning drag from a Camel,
Both pleasures sneered at by the professional class.
My uncle once compared smokers to Jews
In Nazi Germany! The comparison
Was, as the kids would say, "problematic,"
But health can be a form of tyranny,
I guess . . . What was I talking about again?

Ah, yes! Healthful, delicious Coca Cola!
"The Intellectual Drink," "The Ideal Brain Tonic,"
Said to relieve exhaustion and calm the nerves,
To satisfy the thirsty and help the weary.
Like Trump, I drink several cans a day
And sometimes feel powerless with rage.
I'm sorry (sort of) for these affinities
But overwhelmed by social change and struggling
To gain purchase, I've turned to Coca Cola.
On an airplane one time, a woman asked
If I could try to be less animated.

I was relating a story to a friend,
You see, and am excitable by nature.
…Ah, I am exhausted, so exhausted…
Beat down by politics, divorce, and failure,
The past few months have been a son-of-a-bitch.
I'd like the world to buy *me* a Coke, for once,
And keep *me* company. It's the real thing
That I want today, the real thing, the real thing.

VI.

Nobody but You

The park is empty. Nothing moves. Not even
the wind sifting through the trees. Not even
a sleaze in a raincoat. You are alone
in this place. The sidewalks are white. The lamps
are lit for only the grass, the park benches,
a newspaper someone has left, folded,
the crossword puzzle all wrong, filled in
with letters you cannot recognize. Now
the buildings surrounding the park loom
tall and dark. And you think of the city, beyond:
the post office and museums, locked tight.
Security gates down on all the store fronts.
The streets wide and free of cars. A web of houses,
and no lights on in any of them.

Family First

Family first—
                grandfathers most times—
Grow sick and suffer;
                    they show the way.
Our fathers, mothers
                    will falter, fail
At last, give in,
                leave home.
The time is near
                  for tender talk
At bedside vigils,
                  for holding hands.
Days will dead-end,
                    the dark get longer,
Flowers flatten
                finally to dust.
You must believe:
                    To love's to lose.
Sadly, with soft,
                  uneasy light,
Hospitals glow,
                inhuman. Huge.

The First Obscenity

Before we turned our eyes from nudity,
Or banished certain words, death was the first
Obscenity—the one from which the rest,
In time, would find their way. The first
To make a joke of life. The first
To show us what may come of children's games:
A skull left caked in mud, the slicing rain.
What is a rude word if not a reminder
Of the grave in which one's coffin will be lowered?
An old man's kiss upon a young girl's navel
Would not be possible if not for death.

Dressed up in our Sunday best, our deaths
Seem almost hypothetical. They're not.
Plastic surgeons, age-defying creams,
Air-brushed waistlines on the cover of *Cosmo*—
These prove our distaste. Death's in the ghetto.
But only look out past your green kept lawn,
And there it is, unfazed, a grinning fact.

Visiting Hours

I'll admit I stayed away.
We all know it. I prayed.
Sure, I prayed, but stayed away
From you, the shade of what you were.
No one wants to see his brother
That way: shrunken and afraid
Behind a hospital tray. I tried
But couldn't handle it.
I stayed away. Hid from it.
I was afraid. I thought
I might delay what would happen,
The fast-approaching day.

What's there to say? You hit
Some tender spot. You lay there,
Half the weight you used to weigh.
I stayed away. I didn't want to hear
The way your voice was all unmade.
I couldn't stand to think of it.
We'd play blackjack. You'd hardly
Say a word. I shouldn't have been that way,
But how could I convey my love?
You lifted your lids only half-way
To watch the nurse carry
The get-well bouquet away from you.

Rube

Tom, you used to stink of cigarettes.
I'd find you, feet up, smoking in your chair
when I got home from work. The Phillies on.
We'd grunt—if that—for a hello. No need
for anything more formal between brothers.
You loved TV, baseball, and Marlboros.
You were the laziest person I knew.
And now you're gone, gone as Harry Kalas.

But even then your blood was poison, your body
plotting its betrayal with the virus
that, much too soon, would open up the gate
for Death's indifferent agents to slip through.
And I feel like a rube. I always thought
the Marlboros would be what did you in.

My Father's Hands

My small child-hand
    held the hand of my father.
His palm was creased,
    like a well-worn piece of leather.

Calloused in spots
    and burned red from the sun,
my father's hands
    were hands that got things done.

They looked so mighty—
    fleshy and deeply veined—
and seemed to me
    the secret of manhood explained.

But what're my hands?
    They're not my father's kind.
Grown older, not up,
    I feel I'm groping blind.

His finger nails,
    with their small lunar crescents,
come back as his
    and not some convalescent's,

but I tended to them
    once, his hands, then, pale,
atrophied,
    surprisingly so frail.

They hung there limp,
    unable to close or bend—
nor could he speak,
    or even smile, in the end.

Friends Southwestern Burial Ground

The place is loaded up with dead, but still
The low white tombstones hunkered in the grass
Are baby teeth that bear us no ill will.
Its stony wall and gothic fence encompass
A rural oasis tucked among the lanes
Of anxious row homes, corner stores, and taverns.
At night, the brakes of the commuter trains
Screech faintly beneath the screech of its environs.
There, death is made to seem a shutting out
Of all the noise and fuss of dailiness,
And, somehow, we feel more at ease about
The last breath we all have awaiting us.
Outside its gates, this life's so thick with grief
That we can hardly wait for that relief.

Risk

I could break my neck.
My mother was right:
All it takes is one fall.
You could slip backwards
off a porch railing and—Good for you!—
you broke your neck. It's that easy.
She knew. She heard stories.
I could be paralyzed,
take my food through a tube.
Watch your teeth!
If you break these, you don't
get new ones. So help me . . .
And if I ran beside the pool, I could slip
and *skull-fracture* myself.
That was my mother's favorite word:
skull-fracture.

The body bruises so easily.
A girl I knew once had
a purple welt on her thigh
like a new-bloomed crocus in the snow.
I never learned how she got it,
yet it was so *erotic*—And simply because
it emphasized her body's likeness
to a spring-time field of snow, the risk
of danger and pain that makes sex,
even with people you don't love, so interesting.
My mother wouldn't approve.
I'm not sure *I* approve.

And I know I don't approve of my face:
my weak chin and timorous lips,
the ragged way my breath comes,

my heart rattling its cage
after I run to catch a bus.
I don't approve. My brief body . . .

It makes me think of the woman
who takes the stool next to mine
at a deserted bar and asks me
if I have a light. Of course
I shouldn't trust her, her lips
curling into a smile, as she draws
a cigarette slowly from its pack.
It's late. It's always late.
The bar is closing in an hour.
So I lift my lighter and flick the flint.
She leans into the flame.

About the Author

Luke Stromberg's poetry has appeared in *Smartish Pace, The Hopkins Review, The New Criterion, The Philadelphia Inquirer, Golidad Review, Think Journal, The Raintown Review, ONE ART, Cassandra Voices,* and several other venues. He also serves as the Associate Poetry Editor of *E-Verse Radio*. Luke works as an adjunct professor at Eastern University and lives in Upper Darby, Pennsylvania.

www.ingramcontent.com/pod-product-compliance
Lightning Source LLC
Chambersburg PA
CBHW030909170426
43193CB00009BA/787